down the road

by jenn weinshenker

Published by:
Chicago Studio Works
312 83rd Street
Willowbrook, IL

www.chicagostudioworks.com

First Paperback Printing October 2010

All rights reserved.
No part of this book may be reproduced
in any form or by any means, electronic or mechanical,
including photocopying, recording,
or by any information storage and retrieval system,
without the permission in writing from the author,
except in the case of brief quotations
embodied in critical articles or reviews.

Written, printed and manufactured in the USA

Library of Congress Cataloging-in-Publication Data
Jennifer Weinshenker Lieto
down the road
Copyrights Reserved #TXU933484 October 27, 1999

Cover Art and Graphic Design by
Jenn Weinshenker

dedication and acknowledgments

to my precious children
matthew and stephen and rebekah
thank you for all of your help filling in the details
i had forgotten

the substance of this book
would never have taken shape
without you and without your encouragement
loving you and being loved by you
has always been my inspiration

to my amazing sister cynthia
her wonderful husband christopher
and their children chris and katie and kelly
who i love dearly
and to the rest of our incredible family
your every smile and expression of love
reached into my broken heart
and healed me

to my editors: stephen lieto, rebekah lieto, sam allen,
ann whittenkeller, nicole huser, and jude mathews
and to my tech support buds
jake regas, nyq bonaventura and victor yanez
and my dear friends jim jasiak and sarah fell
thank you for peeking out of your busy lives
to give me straight forward advice
during the editing process and publishing of this book
you helped me more than you may ever know

with every breath i breathe
i will forever be grateful
to all of you

Preface

As I read *down the road*, it stirred so many feelings in me. I could picture Jenn's fright as well as her struggle and courage following the accident. The love within her family is a model to others who face adversity. I filled with tears so many times, not from sadness, but from the persistent hope and support they kindled in each other. There were passages that inspired me so much that I read and reread them not only for what they had to say, but for the beauty of the words, as well.

I love to go to a section at random and wrap myself in it. The beauty of Jenn's soul shines through on each page and sends out comforting thoughts of hope and inspiration. Her words are inspiring and lead me to think in feelings, where words are just an adjunct. Her journey has affected me deeply.

Over a long career, I have had the joy of working with individuals who struggle with a variety of challenges, mental and physical. Jenn's personal passage down the road will offer many readers, a perspective of hope, courage and love from someone who has seen challenges from the inside. She continued to search for answers, even when many who should have lead her to answers failed.

Read this book.

Cathryn Weiss, MA
Associate Director
Institute for Teaching and Learning

table of contents

1. whirligig _____ 3
2. the road _____ 6
3. foggy daze _____ 14
4. accident related _____ 21
5. rehab _____ 29
6. soft tissue _____ 34
7. diagnosis _____ 35
8. memory loss _____ 45
9. depression _____ 53
10. changes _____ 59
11. an independent purpose _____ 68
12. a new life _____ 71
13. reading _____ 76
14. music _____ 80
15. writing _____ 84
16. painting _____ 89
17. my senses _____ 92
18. the movies _____ 96
19. a romantic lead _____ 101
20. teaching my children well _____ 103
21. the thought _____ 105
22. the lesson _____ 109
23. acceptance _____ 113
24. spirituality _____ 114
25. the reward _____ 118
26. years later _____ 121

down the road

1. whirligig

it was june 20th
1994

we were driving down blue star highway
i was sitting in the front passenger seat of an old van
enjoying the sounds
of my daughter laughing in the back
and watching the sun streak through
the rich greens of summer
streaming past my window
when out of nowhere
life
curved
and a car brought terror
speeding into our lane

we went off the road to try to get away

oh god

there was an explosion
it was the loudest sound i ever heard
and then a wind
a big wind
and a bright white light came
and took everything away

what happened

i heard rebekah
she sounded so far away
mommy
mommy

she was crying
she needed me

whirligig

there was blood and broken glass everywhere
i could not move my head
could not turn to see her
to see if she was okay
it was bad

are you hurt
come to where i can see you
are you bleeding
take a shirt and hold it on your mouth

i watched as the driver of our van
my second husband
got out
he went to see
what happened to the driver of the car that hit us
the other driver was dead

i could not move
could not think to take off the seat belt
or get out of the van
i was stuck
in too much pain

bekah
is that smoke
it sounded like steam
like pressured air releasing

get out
it's gonna blow
it's gonna blow
we will get hit by a truck
get out get out

she was crying
no

whirligig

no
you have to get out
it's gonna blow

but she wouldn't leave me
at ten years old she was so brave
she stayed
bleeding,
thinking i would die
not caring what happened to her
she stayed

my memory goes blank after that

later i heard
some people went to get help
that lived near a blueberry farm
on the other side of the tree line

later i found out
rebekah was the one who undid my seatbelt
she pulled my body across the engine
and got me out of the van
it was rebekah who was my hero

but the only image i remember started
when i was outside of the van

i was twirling
like some kind of a whirligig
spinning in slow motion
spiraling
toward the ground
falling gently
downward
to a surreal
silent
stop

2. the road

on the side of the road
my body
was tensed with pain
if another car or truck came crashing into us
i could not have moved to save my life
or to save rebekah either

oh god oh god

so much pain
oh god too much

and then
everything got quiet
i felt like i was becoming a part of the breeze
flowing through the leaves and weeds

i was going out to everywhere
and whatever made me who i was
that made me different from being the road or a tree
took me through its boundaries
and carried me through all of those in between spaces
to where it was peaceful and free

ah

and then
i heard rebekah calling me
mommy mommy
yes bekah
mommy
she was crying
i wanted to reach for her
no use
could not move

the road

all i wanted to do was stay with her
and not leave her
and comfort and hold her
we laid there on the road
together
until lights flashed my eyes shut
and they took me away

i could not understand what was happening
everything was confusing and muffled

too bright
too fast

cold metal

help

breathe

where is rebekah
someone kept saying stay with us

i heard bekah's voice
coming from somewhere out there
she sounded like a little bell far away
like a ringing little bell
singing into my heart
live
i need you
live mommy
i love you

oh god
pain
i went from one place to another
terrified tubes would be put down my throat
terrified doctors would cut on me
and i would know it

the road

a nurse told me to pee in a cup
then she disappeared behind some glass or a curtain
her steps down that hall echoed all of my hopes
someone was going to help me
but when she came back she glared at me and said
you'd better pee in that cup or i'll put a catheter in you

i was already so afraid
in so much pain
she did not know
to her i was taking too much time
being difficult
i smiled and tried to pee
i was telling my body what to do
but it wasn't listening
i was nervous and in so much pain
the thought of more
made me panic

my sister cynthia got me something to drink
finally enough ran out of me for the sample cup
brain swelling did not show up in my urine
i guess they figured i was okay
because they sent me home

someone said my blood gasses were okay
temperature was okay too
later the one story brick country clinic released me
i have no memory of leaving

i did not know how lucky we were
that rebekah was alive and that i had my legs
until some time later
when we went to see the van

it looked like a bomb had gone off in the back of the van
the custom built bench where rebekah was resting
her head propped up on a pillow as she read
was splintered chaos

the road

there was this tiny triangle where
my legs must have been trapped
metal was crushed in all around this tiny little triangle
one of my sandals was stuck in the metal
my eyes welled up
i was overcome and began to cry
how could my legs have fit in there
bekah said they didn't
your other leg was over and behind
the big hump of metal
between the front seats
your back was laying on top of it

oh

someone explained later that the car that hit us
was going down the two lane highway
some where between 55 and 80 miles per hour
there weren't any skid marks
which meant the driver never put on his brakes

the force of the crash
sent our ¾ ton van up into the air
then the van flew back from the car that hit us
and we landed about ten feet away
when the van came crashing down on its nose
the rear rocked so hard
it slammed the back of the van onto the ground
with so much force i was sure another car had hit us
but it hadn't
it was the sudden stop back down to earth i felt

that day on his way home
the same late afternoon sun streaked through
the other driver's windows too
he left behind his wife and three small children
investigators figured alcohol or drugs wasn't a factor
maybe he had a heart attack or a stroke
or he might have fallen asleep at the wheel

the road

he had been working a lot of overtime
i heard he and his wife were saving
to open a pastry shop in town

when the accident happened
my boys were in new york visiting their dad
matt had turned thirteen the year before
and had decided to go live with his dad for awhile
he wanted a chance to get to know him better
that was the first year the boys had ever been a part
they were missing each other
they wanted to spend some
male bonding time together
so steve left a couple of weeks earlier
and rebekah was set to join them upstate soon

the day of the crash
matt was graduating the eighth grade
when he got the news
your mom and your sister have been in an accident
you'd better go home
he ran all of the way
not knowing if we were alive or dead

my sister must have called the boys
i remember hearing their sweet voices
and thinking
maybe i will never see my sons again

no

that was too much
that could not happen
i had to see them again

hearing the voices of my children
calling me
gave me hope

the road

they were my lifeline
their love kept me from sinking
into the confusion and pain
and filled me with the strength and determination
to survive

gritting through the indescribable pain
had created an unusual comfort
when i thought about dying as an alternative
to what i was living through
it all seemed like such a quiet welcome relief
and yet i willed
to hear rebekah's voice
to see matt and steve and hold them again
and to see their smiling eyes once more

they were so young
they would have been so sad
being left like that
it was unthinkable

i had to keep trying to get better

when the boys came home that summer
they did not know how bad things were
none of us did
they were relieved to hear i was alive
they thought everything must be okay
no broken bones
the hospital let me go
so everything must have been okay

but everything wasn't okay

i got lost in my mind
in all that pain
and there i stayed

the road

without good insurance or a doctor who knew me
i was left to the mercy and suspicion of the very people
i relied on for my survival
at the time i didn't understand why this was so
but i felt it and it was very disturbing

while all of this was going on
pain kept slamming me head on
back to reality
i knew
there was no way my body could hold
all of that pain
eventually it would break through
and then it did
i started shaking all over
cold gripped me
right through my bones
i went to an emergency room
i do not remember what they did
they did not know what was wrong
they did not know my brain was swelling
brain swelling did not give me a temperature
brain swelling did not show up
in my blood gasses either
it could not be seen by shining a light into my eyes
i think they gave me a shot
they did not understand how serious
the accident had been
they sent me home
i think this was when someone referred me
to the brain injury department of the hospital

during this time rebekah was in terrible bad pain
her back was completely bruised
and she was black and blue
on one side of her body from top to bottom
her nose was broken and her lip was cut
her face was also bruised and swollen

the road

as her little body slowly began to heal
she tried her best to get on with everyday life
but i could see
she was becoming increasingly frustrated
i could see
the fear in her eyes
i told the doctors my daughter wasn't the same
she was in pain
but no one listened and
no one helped her

that summer
rebekah met up with her dad and brothers
on crutches
and i stayed inside thinking
one day maybe
maybe one day
i won't wake up anymore
and this will all be over

one day maybe
maybe one day
i will wake up and be back to myself again

but that one day never came
a part of me stayed on that patch of road
in those trees
and i never got it back

down the road

3. foggy daze

day to day living and much of the past
was lost in a fog i could not see through
one day was like the last or the next
my emotions were one long flat line

why wasn't i happy to be alive
it did not make any sense
why was i so

remote

daytime was too bright
at night it was too dark
going away from the inside of the house
was unsteady without reason

when i got out of a car after it stopped
or when the ground was uneven
or when the wind swirled things up in the air
i felt like i was moving through
invisible currents of water
the ground moved like beach sand
under my feet
and everything
the walls
even the trees outside looked
wavy

when i walked
every step felt like i was walking on
open metal lotus flowers
each time i put my foot down
intense pain shot up through my body

lightly i would go

foggy daze

you can make it
sit down
sit down soon

if it was a bad day
where i did too much
and walked too far
or when life moved around me too much
i clomped around like a two year old
and was bent and crippled
unable to control my body

loud static ringing
louder than the tv or people talking
filled my head
i could not get used to
the constant noise inside my head
ear plugs didn't help
putting a pillow over my head didn't help either
at night when the house was quiet
i felt like banging my head against the wall
i wanted to crack it open
to let the noise out

it was so strange
one day i was enjoying the sound of a breeze
and birds in the trees
and the next day
a loud buzzing and ringing
shoved all of that peace and quiet
out of my mind
and just like that
it was gone

weeks turned into months
and i still could not make sense out of words
i could not follow recipes
or move fast
or stand balanced

foggy daze

i could not dry my hair with my head down
handle watching tv
or listen to music
i could not go to the movies
or have a long talk on the phone
i could not keep track of conversations
or stay awake
i dropped things and broke dishes
and stubbed my toes so many times some broke

getting ready to start the day
took all of my effort and energy
when i took a shower
i forgot
did i already wash my hair
when i finished washing my hair
i wondered
did i bathe yet
and then
i forgot
about everything
and just let the water run down
the back of my head and neck
and felt grateful for hot water and a clean bathtub
and i relaxed

the really hard part to getting ready
for the day came next
when i looked in the mirror
it felt like a stranger was looking back at me
through my eyes
i wanted to throw something at it
and tell it to go away
but i was afraid to break the glass

then i'd walk over to the cabinet
did i brush my teeth already
wait a minute

foggy daze

i reached for the toothpaste just in case
a dark cloud of confusion and panic
rolled into my mind
what am i doing here
am i putting this toothpaste away
or do i need to brush my teeth
i had no idea what i was doing
or why i was standing there

when my family or old friends talked about
things we had done together
places we had gone
or homes we used to live in
it was like they were talking about someone else's life
there were no moving picture memories in my mind
even when we looked at family photos
no memories came back
i didn't even recognize myself in those pictures

some times out of the stillness of my mind
fractured images would appear
like random snapshots pulled out of a box
that belonged to someone else
i felt no connection to them

doing simple things like grocery shopping
with all of those bright lights and big sale signs
and carts and screeching wheels
and an endless stream of wavy shelves
just wore me out
i forgot what i needed by the time i walked
down the first aisle of the store
i bought things that looked familiar
if i needed something
i might buy it every week for a month
i would have five mustards crammed on the shelves
and still no ketchup
i could not figure out

foggy daze

what was wrong with me

when i got home
i could not handle thinking about
all of this life anymore
i fell into a deep sleep
and when someone needed to wake me
i woke up gasping for air
shaking
like i was being pulled out of deep water

i do not remember how long it was
before i tried to drive
or went grocery shopping
or made a phone call
all i do remember is that everything i tried
took all of my strength
and left me drained

when i tried to do something normal
like drive
i got lost
stopping at a traffic light
or kids walking across the street
was all the distraction i needed
to lose all sense of my direction

and hearing a siren echo through the streets
that made me loose it completely

when a car passed a truck
and came into my lane
i had to pull over
my heart was pounding so fast
all i could think was this is it
i am going to have a heart attack
inside i screamed
help

foggy daze

and then i whispered
breathe
take it easy

where am i
where am i going
panic took over again

breathe

once i calmed down
i stopped and asked for directions
but by the time i turned around and walked to the car
i had forgotten everything
so i went back into the gas station
would you mind writing the directions down for me
and please
even if going in straight lines takes longer
make it simple
oh and i need to stay off the highway
it got so i did not want to go anywhere alone
because i always got lost
it was embarrassing

fear slowly crept into my mind
i was terrified i was going to get into another accident
i was weak and in trouble and
aware there were people who would
take advantage of this weakness and hurt me

i was terrified a doctor would find out what was wrong
and want to drill a hole in my head or operate on my back
i was afraid they would not find out what was wrong
and i would be left undone

i was worried if people knew how hard things were for me
someone might take away my children
so for a while i kept my thoughts and worries to myself
i waited for a moment of peace and quiet

foggy daze

the same way i waited for each night to pass
hoping tomorrow i would feel better
but the next day only brought
more of the same
no matter what i did
or how long i waited
normal
was gone

my life
was now
as is

down the road

4. accident related

before the accident i was a healthy young
writer and an artist
and a house painter
and i also worked part-time jobs
so i would be home for my kids after school
i was writing a book
and finishing a painting in a series of oils
called the faces of a woman
i had gotten remarried
and i was the mother of three terrific kids
our lives were our own

we had enough money to live on
but medical insurance was too expensive
so i was without coverage
if i got sick
i did not go to a doctor
i just got over it

after the accident
my life was turned upside down
even though i needed a doctor
it was almost impossible to see one
without a referral or medical insurance

when i called a doctor's office
the person making appointments
would ask me
do you have insurance
yes
and then i told them the name of the car insurance
were you in an accident
yes
do you have any other insurance
no
do you have a primary doctor

accident related

no
do you have a referral
no
sorry, the doctor isn't taking any new patients
click
days passed before i was up for trying again
do you have medical insurance
sorry
click

someone helped me find a doctor
who was taking new patients
the only problem was
he had the initials *do* at the end of his name not *md*
it was my impression that the car insurance company
did not like that
it was also my impression that a lot of the special doctors
would not take referrals from my doctor
because they did not take him seriously
he helped as much as he could
he was a nice man
he was a chiropractor doctor
he worked on my back and neck
it was very bad painful and did not help
the last time he adjusted my neck
my whole body launched into the air
it was as though my body had become a flat board
which felled no differently
than a slab of lumber on hard earth
when it hit the table

during that first year
before people knew what was wrong with me
a lot of my problems were said back to me
like they were little
oh ringing in your ears can happen after an accident
no one knew how loud the noise was
until i was tested nearly two years later

accident related

another time a shopping mall eye doctor said don't worry
a lot of people your age
start to have problems with their vision
medical people said
you are bound to be achy and sore
you were in a bad car accident

when i complained about my memory problems
people told me not to worry
i forget things all the time too
then they made a joke about the last time
they forgot something
when i tried to explain how hard it was to drive
how terrifying it was getting lost
people said you get lost
because you haven't lived here that long
sometimes i heard stories about how much
they hated getting lost too
these were my words of comfort
from those i hoped would help me

looking back through medical reports the dates showed
it took a year to get to a special eye doctor
that knew about brain injuries
it took one year and four months
to get to an oral surgeon about my jaw
it took a year and seven months to get to
a special nose and ears doctor

it took more than a year before
my first brain injury doctor's
initial dictation tapes were transcribed
it took a year and three months
before my other doctors and rehab got those reports

it took a little over two years to see another special doctor
at the university of michigan in ann arbor
i never did see a heart doctor

accident related

or had tests run to find out
why i felt like a heavy bag of pudding was laying
just below the surface of my skin
and all down the left side of my chest

i remember asking once during
an ultrasound of my pelvis
could you take an image a little higher too
maybe it will show why i am still in so much pain
near my heart
it's aim was only a hand away from the truth
the lady giving the test
looked like she was going to cry
they could only do what the doctor ordered
she was very sorry i was in so much pain

i had told my doctor
for the past two months
since the accident
i could barely go to the bathroom
my belly was swollen and shiny
and i was in terrible pain

he told me that was impossible

another doctor told me my heart may have been bruised
there had been soft tissue damage
around my ribcage and collar bone
i could not understand why seeing a good doctor
or having tests taken early enough after the accident
to find out what was wrong
was such a struggle

later i thought maybe
the insurance company did not want tests run
that would prove i had problems
then i thought maybe
the insurance company did not want to pay for tests
if the results would not prove

accident related

what they found was accident related
maybe
it was hard to get help
because i had been released
from that first emergency room
or maybe it was because people
who should have been watching out for me
weren't

all i knew was that i wasn't supposed to worry
the insurance company and doctors and lawyer
were supposed to take good care of me
but i found out
what is supposed to happen and reality
is not always the same thing

doctors did not want to get involved with a patient
if their bills were not going to be paid
i could not blame them for that
no one works for free

and my lawyer
well i was probably worth more
dead than alive to him anyway
whatever the reason
i don't think he ever really heard me

so who really cared
whether i lived or died

i was caught in a system
that suspected everyone
and cared for no one
i had to depend on the very same people
who had everything to gain
by not helping me
to get the medical attention i needed
and that worry was the reality i lived through every day

accident related

oh sure the insurance company promised
they would always
pay for medicine
and pay for doctors
and pay for anything i needed
as long as it was accident related
and the cost was what they considered
to be a reasonable amount
and as long as the reports were in their office
and and and
they made everything so complicated i gave up
it was nearly impossible to get them to
pay the medical bills
or pay for the medicines i needed

it seemed like they were trying to get out of
paying for doctors and the tests the doctors ordered
all of the time

they did not care collection notices came to my house
they did not care my credit was ruined
they did not care i was all upset
they did not care about the pain i was in
because of the stress
and i could not deal with any of it
not the bills
not the paperwork
or the appointments

i felt devalued and thought
what if i die from all of the strain
these worries are putting on my mind
and then i realized
it did not matter if anyone else cared
if i lived or died
i had to go on living for my children

accident related

life was spinning
more and more out of focus
and i could not stop it
i could not fight for myself and
i could not hold onto memories or thoughts
long enough to figure out
what my problems were
all i could do was ask for help
and for a long time i did
only no one listened

the lawyer wanted me to sue everybody
but it did not make sense to me to widen
the pool of tragedy and hardship

the little country clinic was needed there
what good would it have done to sue them
the employer of the man who hit us
while driving a company car
wasn't to blame for what happened
why sue him
what good would that do

settlements had been capped in michigan
so after the lawyer took his third
and my soon to be ex took his third and left
i figured we had enough money
to move some where quiet
and hopefully it would last long enough
to see my kids graduate high school
i had a life insurance policy
in case i died and that was about as far as
my ability to plan for the future went

it was clear we needed to make some changes
so i decided to stop the insanity
if the insurance company
wasn't going to pay for medicine

accident related

and did not care how
collections from a pharmacy worried me
i would just quit taking the medicine
if the insurance company
wasn't going to pay doctor bills
or pay for the tests the doctors ordered
i would stop going to see doctors

and so for a while i stopped asking for help
and tried very hard to be strong
like i used to be

down the road

5. rehab

communicating with the people at rehab was hard
the first rehab place i went to did not help very much
a lady who worked there got mad at me
she said i would get better
if i did not sleep on the couch all day
someone else said
you were not in a coma
you can't be sleeping so much
you can't have all of these problems

things got better when i went to see dr.hoyt
he changed where i went to rehab
it was there that i started working with
dr. denman my nuero-psyche
and my occupational and physical therapists
lynne and deb to name a few

in the beginning it was still hard
to tell people what they wanted to know
i had forgotten so much of my life

i was slow
and when they asked me out of the blue stuff
i had nothing
no memory at all
it must have been hard for the people at rehab
to understand me too
when someone asked me a question
i would answer that question
only maybe there were other things i needed to say
that would make everything clear
but i could not think of everything
all at once anymore
things had to be spelled out for me

i did not understand any in between the lines stuff

rehab

if i was asked about my education
i wrote down that i had gone to college for three years
i knew this was true
because i found the paper that said so
only i forgot that my last name was different back then
so when the insurance investigators
wanted to see my school records
there weren't any
when i was questioned about that i felt like
these people think i tried to trick them
i did not know what to do
it was a nightmare

i knew i needed help
that was all i knew for sure
so when i went to my next appointment
i brought my passport and school papers
and marriage and divorce papers and birth certificates
and every thing else in my important papers box
and pictures of me before the accident
pictures of the crashed van
and any other papers i could find
that would show who i was
then they knew
i wasn't leaving things out about my life on purpose
i did not remember them

for two years people tested my brain
strangers documented all of my flaws
and at the end of the day
when everyone went home to be with their families
i was left exhausted
and feeling like a claim number in an open file
that belonged to the insurance company

my privacy was gone
and it all gave me the creeps

rehab

eventually the rehab people understood
where the brain damage was
and that was when i began to learn
how to compensate
for my areas of weakness
they encouraged me to work hard
and i did
i was determined to get
as much of my life back as possible

some days were better than others
but most of the time i felt fragile
and broken

one day i was waiting in a room during rehab
when tears started to roll down my face
i must have been in a lot of pain
i did not want to cry or complain
but when the rehab lady saw me there
she was moved and
she held me
and it hit me
someone cared and felt bad i was in pain
and that was a comfort to me

i began to have faith in the kindness of people again

the people at rehab had compassion in their hearts
they helped me find a way to do artwork again
they helped me figure things out
those people had nothing to gain by helping me
they were going to get paid
no matter how much i learned
or how my tests turned out
or even how my life turned out
they taught me how to slow down
slow down to talk
so i would not stutter or say my words wrong
slow down to walk

rehab

so i would not fall and get hurt
they helped me use a cane for balance
so people would not try to hurry me across the street
so i would not fall down in the road
trying to be normal
so i would go outside again

before the accident reading and writing
were the strongest and most natural parts
of my thinking life
after the accident they were the most frustrating
every failed effort
every hour of pain after ten minutes of trying to read
only to forget what i had read
was emotionally so painful
that i did not even want to try
the rehab people helped me to keep trying
they helped me understand i needed to be patient
so my ability to read and write would improve

rehab taught me i needed to live simply
instead of cooking a main dish and vegetables and
homemade biscuits and pie
i needed to learn how to make one-dish meals
and some times if i was tired
i needed to use a box of ready mix
or heat up some frozen food

at rehab i learned to have confidence
that what i saw was real
i learned how to deal with reality
and understand and trust my feelings
i learned how to stand up for myself and ask for help
i learned how to expect less and accept more
and i learned how to never give up

the rehab people and doctors that cared saved my life
together they figured out what was wrong
they helped me learn new ways of doing things

rehab

they encouraged me and said kind words to me
and they helped me find a purpose in living again

through the recovery process
they were gentle and honest when they explained
why i was having problems
they respected my spirituality and
helped me feel engaged with life again
and that was meaningful

6. soft tissue

i had a lot of soft tissue injuries
i did not know what that meant until much later
when a doctor showed me a bowling ball
he said think of the bowling ball like it was your head
then with his hands
he looked like he was going to throw the ball
then he pulled the ball back the other way real fast
he did that a few times up and down and back to front
he said my head was like that bowling ball
being thrown back and forth
from the force of the accident
he explained that my body had been
pulled and twisted and shaken too
more violently than i could imagine
stretching the muscles and tendons and cartilage
that were holding me all together
that was what caused the nose cartilage to dislodge
that was why it was so hard to hold my head upright
that was why my posture was slouched
and that was why my jaw was now out of line

other doctors told me soft tissue injuries
were the reason it was so hard to walk
and why my joints were loose
they had been weakened and strained
and that was why it was so hard to lift or carry things
and it was why i dropped things

the cartilage had pulled away from my ribcage
and other bones all over my body too
and that was why my body hurt all over

all of the inside workings that had spent a life time
growing together cell by cell
were bruised and hyper extended
and most of that damage
was permanent

7. diagnosis

for a long time rebekah
had bad stomach pain when she rode in a car
especially on the highway
she wanted to move to an island up north
where there weren't any cars allowed
she got frustrated easily
and it was painful for her
to sit at her desk at school
her hips and wrists and ankles popped
and walking was very painful for her

bekah had to relearn multiplying and dividing
which was hard for her and often made her cry
about a year and a half after the accident
the insurance company okayed some tests
but by the time they finally did
too much time had passed
a doctor said she was probably in so much pain
because of soft tissue injuries
loose joints and bruised bones
he told us her bruised bones
could take two or three years to heal
no these things did not show up on an x-ray
she will be okay he told us
kids bounce back
the bills for the doctor and those tests
went into collection too

the lack of care rebekah received
and the absence of help offered to all of the kids
adjusting to a parent with a brain injury
was shameful
there wasn't any help for us as a family
we were on our own

diagnosis

all this time i kept thinking i was going to wake up
and live free again
but the more time that went by
the more i knew i needed help
i had to accept that even though
i did not want to need help
i could not take good care of my family
or myself
without it

it was a frustrating time
doctors and rehab people would ask me
why are you here today
and i would tell them
i don't know
everything has been different since the accident
why
i don't know
what is wrong
i don't know
i thought you were going to tell me what was wrong

two months after the accident
i had gone to an obgyn clinic for my yearly
i was still in a lot of pain in my belly
and still having trouble going to the bathroom
the doctor ran a test and found
i had epithelial cell abnormality and
atypical squamous cells of
undetermined significance
then he ordered a pelvic ultrasound
the results showed a complex adenaxel mass
which the report said
could have been among other things
a hematoma which could have been due to
a hemorrhage or internal bleeding
he scheduled me for another echo pelvic exam
in two weeks

diagnosis

before that next appointment
i went to the bathroom and flushed
some black syrupy looking stuff
that took about an hour to empty out of me
it was painless
i never knew what it was
but after that i could go to the bathroom again

my follow up scan revealed
no dysplastic or malignant cells were seen
in regards to the large complex mass
previously described
it is not evident
if there was no surgery since the last exam
perhaps it was a distended loop of bowel
adjacent to the ovary

around this time i went to see dr. hoyt
he was the first real brain injury doctor to see me
he listened and was very gentle with me
i finally felt like someone understood and cared
about what was wrong with me

and then a few months later i got a call from his office
you will be seeing a new doctor
why
dr. hoyt has died of a brain aneurysm
what
and just like that he was gone

i thought about him
his kind eyes looking into mine
searching for answers to the puzzle in my brain
he valued my life
he must have valued all of life

he asked questions i understood
he waited for me to answer
before asking me another question

diagnosis

if he wasn't sure i understood the question
he would go slow and ask me again
until i understood what he wanted to know
he tried to understand what i told him
he was the perfect example
of a great humanitarian
he was so young
i was going to miss his smile
i felt sad for his family
knowing they would miss him too

the death of dr. hoyt was a shock
i felt so alone again
and couldn't help but wonder
how could this happen
could this happen to me
our lives were so fragile
so uncertain
and then i grieved

a temporary doctor took over for him
he was supposed to take care of me
until they found a new doctor
to be the head of the brain injury department
it took him about a year before he knew
who i was or what was in my file
eventually he did send me to some good doctors
the eye doctor he referred me to
discovered that i was seeing double
and that my eyes could not see center anymore
he also found that my eyes were not scanning
when there was movement around me
or when i was moving
and that was why images had become
complicated and strange
and he found out my eyes were extremely sensitive
to light or sudden changes in lighting

diagnosis

about this time the doctors and rehab people
met with me around a big table
they explained that nerves were stretched
and some were torn
my mid-brain wasn't communicating change fast enough
and that was why i was permanently out of focus

almost a year and a half after the accident
the special nose and ears doctor i went to
found that the cartilage
holding my nose to the bone had come off
and attached itself to the inside of my nose
closing off one of my nasal passages
and that was why it had been so hard to breathe
he also discovered i had problems with my inner ear
which effected my balance
so the more activity around me
the more disabled my walking became

he also found out
that i had true vertigo and tinnitus
and my brain wasn't processing
the difference between
noises that were close and those that were far away
so when different sounds came together
what i heard was a distortion
sometimes i heard a giant moth
flying by my ear
and it was so real i ducked down to get out of it's way
other times i heard what sounded like
a helicopter landing on the roof
but the truth was there weren't any
giant moths in the living room
or helicopters landing on the roof
it was probably just a car going past the house

the oral surgeon i had seen a year and a half
after the accident wrote i was suffering from
craniomandibular/cervical disorders

diagnosis

with myofascial pain and
temporomandibular joint trauma
contributing to etiology
trauma that was caused by the stretching
and tearing of the ligaments of the
temporomandibular joint
and this may never heal
he helped me to understand why
holding my head up without support was so hard

two years after the accident
i went to see another brain injury doctor
his name was dr. telian
his eyes were so smart
i could almost see him thinking
he was the director of the otology/neurology division
at the medical school at the university of michigan
he had me plugged up to these machines
they ran electrical tests
with these plugs all over my body and head
mapping out how the nerves in my brain
communicated with the rest of me
these tests confirmed
what the other doctors and rehab people had observed

my brain stem had been damaged in the accident
reports said i had multi-sensory processing deficits
central nervous system dysfunction
with residual dorsal column and cerebella deficits
true vertigo and tinnitus
and decreased appropriate perception
and convergence insufficiency exophoria
and a compound myopic astigmatism
and residual motor apraxia and presbyopia
what all of those long words
in the medical reports meant
i couldn't understand

diagnosis

all i knew was
i could not be fixed

several years later a doctor
took an mri of my head neck and back
he told me my back had been broken
arthritis had developed in a straight line
where the fracture had occurred

fourteen years after the accident
i was tested at the chicago lighthouse
dr. squier discovered i had peripheral blindness
my eyes were visually capable of seeing
but the information wasn't being processed in my brain
she also found that my brain wasn't recognizing
contrast and depth very well
this was because of permanent nerve damage
and could not be cured
but they could help me with strategies
and give me an understanding
of what was happening to me
so i could hold onto my independence

my occupational therapist hillary
came out to my house
she helped me understand how this affected my life
i used to waste so much of my time and energy
searching for things
the phone, my bag, the leash
at the time they were all black
so my brain couldn't differentiate them
from what they were next to or set on

just knowing that when i set something down
if it was dark i needed to put it on something light
or to put brightly colored tape on things
wound up making my life so much easier
she also got me a good portable task lamp
and good wrap around sun glasses

diagnosis

that helped minimize
the blinding reaction i had
when light changed when i went inside or out

and thanks to my amazing new primary care doctor
i was referred to a very smart orthopedic doctor
dr. vargo x-rayed my ankles and feet
she found that i had paresis post brain injury
with instability and hind foot varus
my ankles were tilting forward
and the arches of my feet now sloped out sideways
she explained that with some brain injured people
these things were seen
my brain wasn't reading where my ankles
or where my feet were accurately
which caused a lot of balance problems and pain
and changed the way my body held my frame upright
and this was one of the reasons i used to
clomp so much when i walked
and why i still do when i am tired or out of focus

i was also referred to a local ear doctor
who explained that the often high pitched
and always buzzing sound in my head
was brain noise
the connection between some of the
transmitters in my brain
and their receptors had been broken
without these receivers connecting
their messages would endlessly ricochet
inside my head
searching for a compatible pathway
to hitch itself too

i had been telling a doctor i used to see
for about seven years
that my heart felt like it was fluttering
and that i had a couple of really bad headaches

diagnosis

so bad i felt like i was going to die
a feeling i had some experience with before
i showed him these little red dots
on my upper chest and neck area
that appeared the next day after those
bad headaches
i asked why they never went away
he couldn't explain it
curiously when i went to see him
my blood pressure always read low

thanks to my social worker emily
at the chicago lighthouse
i finally opened up and talked
about my heart and health concerns
and the sense that my doctor wasn't listening to me
she urged me to get a primary care doctor
being on medicare i wasn't sure i could get one
but i knew i needed to see someone who
had good communication skills

i finally got a really good primary care doctor
he discovered that my blood pressure was high
through using a blood pressure machine at home
and going in for regular exams
and having a few scans and an echo cardiogram
and blood work done
dr. stephan explained to me
that i have had high blood pressure
for an extended period of time
and as a result my heart was enlarged
and this may be why i was feeling
more lightheaded and out of breath
oh and those little red dots
they were from broken capillaries
blood vessels
which probably happened
from spikes in my blood pressure

diagnosis

then i realized
i used to take an anti-stress pill
before i went to see my other doctor in the city
because i still couldn't handle
being in a car on the highway
and his office was about an hour away
which was probably why my blood pressure
appeared low all of those years i saw him
and why my high blood pressure
may have been missed

i have made a few changes in my diet
and now that i have these great orthotics for my shoes
prescribed by dr. vargo
i can walk longer with my service dog coco
so hopefully this will help
with the problems i am dealing with now

explanations through the years have been comforting
even if no one could make me all better
it was always good to know there were reasons
why my head and back and feet hurt so much
and why my balance was off
and why i was so weak and couldn't do very much

it took a few years
for the doctors and test results
to define the new me
understanding the impact
these diagnoses would have on my life
took quite a bit longer

down the road

8. memory loss

getting used to living
without reference
was difficult
my memory only held
disconnected
mosaic images
floating against a black backdrop
there were no emotions or details
binding them together
to give them meaning

whatever just happened
and most of the things that took place
a long time ago
had simply disappeared
i was without context
i felt like a ghost walking through my life

time meant nothing to me anymore
when the sun was out it was day
when the sky was dark
it was time to be inside
leaves changing color
meant it was fall
snow on the ground
must be winter
new sprouts in fresh moist soil
and buds on the trees
it was spring
and long days with ripe vegetables in the garden
meant it was summer
but if you asked me what month it was
or what day it was
without a calendar handy
i had no idea

memory loss

keeping track of where the children were
was another challenge
when one of their friends called
to ask where the kids were
all i could think was
good question
they were not in the house
it was too quiet
but where were they
how long had they been gone
had they asked to stay at a friend's house
were they coming home in a little while
i didn't know
confusion churned inside my head
without a connection to my past or present
my life didn't make sense

why did i forget my entire childhood
and remember the tree outside my bedroom window

when i was a young girl i must have had friends over
i must have had slumber parties
yet i remembered nothing in particular
the only picture i had in my mind
was of the sun coming in through my window
and the view of the yard and this massive old tree
and that was it
there were no images of what my room looked like
i did not know what color my room was
or what the furniture looked like
i just remembered the tree outside my bedroom window

i had a vague memory
of my grandma standing in my room
she was holding something and looking at me
the impression that was left
was that she found an outfit she had given me
on the floor of my closet

memory loss

and i had hurt her feelings by being so careless
but i could not remember our conversation

clearly i had learned how to be gracious
and responsible when given a gift
and i always put my clothes away
so the life lesson had remained

i knew my grandma was fearless and wise
and the most incredible philosopher i had ever known
i knew she taught me how to love the written word
and she encouraged me to think for myself
but the only visual memory i had left of her
was of that moment when she stood in my room
and looked at me with those hurt eyes

when i thought of my best friend sarah
i saw a still picture of her sitting in a chair
with a bag full of lemons
biting through the skin to peel it
she was pregnant with jessica and she was so happy
and that one visual image was what remained
from all of our years being best friends

i had only one childhood memory of my sister
we were playing with dolls
sitting under our dining room table doll house
nothing else was attached to the memory
no sound
no movement
no words
just a still picture of the sun
coming in through the window
behind her
where we played
and that was it

memory loss

my mom had been a successful business woman
so it was strange that the only visual memory i had of her
was during this one summer day
when we were washing cupboards
at our old lake house in michigan
she was explaining
how she found pleasure in taking something dull
and making it shine
it must have made a strong impression
because throughout my life
whenever i cleaned something
i heard my mom say
this is my canvas

somehow i knew we had enjoyed going to the city
and museums and concerts and ravinia park
and i knew we had
interesting discussions in our living room
i just did not remember what our living room looked like

in time i learned
none of that old stuff mattered anymore
it was the past
i did not want to waste time
fretting over a past i could not remember
or miss today
because i was looking too far down the road
this moment right now was all i needed
it did not matter that i was living in an unknown world
where the only one who did not know
what was going on was me
what mattered was i was living
and for that i was very grateful

i joined in the conversation of life again
by accepting the limitations
that went along with memory loss
instead of *not* talking about the life
i could not remember

memory loss

instead of nodding and saying oh yes
when my family and friends talked about something
that happened in the past
that i did not remember
i asked questions about what they remembered
and that was how we relived the memory
together
through their eyes

during our everyday lives
the kids and i learned that i was directed
by whatever was visually in front of me
i couldn't follow a schedule
or remember oral instructions anymore
and i could not take care of
the housework and cooking like before
if the table had dust on it then it got dusted
if the floor was dirty then it was cleaned
i could not plan my week out
you know laundry one day and cleaning another
because i never knew what day it was
the rehab people taught me how to use visual cues
like calendars and dry ink boards on the refrigerator
so i could keep track of
where everybody was
and what i needed to do that day or that week

there were also some strange effects to our lives
because of the way i moved through the day
by what visually stimulated me
we realized this the most when we were in a store
the kids would tell me to stay here
we'll be right back
don't ditch us mom

what
when did i ever ditch you

memory loss

mom when we go shopping and we tell you
stay here
i will be right back
i am just going over there to get something
and you always say ok
but as soon as we are gone
you ditch us

no way

yes way
you do that all of the time

when they said this
i could see them looking at each other
replaying the countless times i had ditched them
and i was shocked
we talked it through
and figured out what probably happened

while i was waiting for them
i started looking at things on the shelves
maybe there was something interesting down the aisle
so i went to look at it
and before long i was all of the way over
on the other side of the store
forgetting where i was and what i was doing there
just kind of moving right along
thinking how do i get out of here
have i been lost for a long time
maybe i should ask for help
what should i say
and it was usually at that moment
when one of the kids would appear
hey mom
what are you doing all of the way over here
by bike tires and golf clubs

oh just looking around

memory loss

mom
you don't realize it but your a shorty
and when you start walking down aisles
we can't see you
you disappear when we are in stores all of the time

oh i do not

ok whatever

do i
do i really

yeah mom
you really do that
all of the time

i felt bad but oh what a laugh we had that day
the things we have had to get used to

we also learned that visual cues
helped me regain a sense of what my interests were
when i saw a cassatt or renoir a picasso or monet
i knew i loved their paintings

i knew i loved shakespeare and frost and
service and dylan
when i saw their books on my shelves

i knew i loved patchouli oil and incense
and india prints
when i went into a store that sold those items

and i knew i loved bogart and bacall
the old black and white movies and musicals
because of my video collection

memory loss

when i looked at my old sheet music
i knew i had studied piano much of my life
i knew bach was perfection
beethoven was passion and mozart was genius
but i just could not tell you why

the constant flow of ideas or images
that had once been my stream of consciousness
had become a dark quiet place

unless i saw
a painting or a book on the shelf or an old movie
or a cd cover that looked familiar
i did not think about anything
not artists   writers films or music

and yet somehow
without reason
visual cues brought traces of my life back

my brain worked differently now
i accepted that and began to appreciate being
simple minded
the gentle qualities
i had yearned for all of my life
had after all become
my new and cherished
separate reality

9. depression

the doctors did not want me to be depressed
they gave me pills
to keep me from
thinking too much
to keep me from
feeling too much
and they gave me these little yellow plastic boxes
to put them in
to keep me from
taking too much

i could not understand why they were so worried
being depressed made perfect sense
when nothing else about my life was making any

during those first two years
there were just these mysterious impressions
from a blank past
half thoughts
unspoken truths and unanswered questions
floating around in my brain

sometimes i had these random realizations
and when i tried to express one of those thoughts
i would get almost to the whole point
and then
complete blackness
memory loss would slam shut
to silence
my computer shut down
the screen went blank
there was no spark
no electricity
that wasn't depression
that was
different

depression

some times i worried about
what was going to happen next
would my children be okay
would i live through all of this
would i wind up in a wheel chair
would i ever get my life back
and for a while those questions
became the ink that defined me
and the darkness that moved through me
every day and every endless night

would i want to survive
without a purpose
what was my reason to live
what was my value
if i could not raise my own children
if i could not work

how could i dream about the future
when i could not imagine one

thinking i might wind up in a wheel chair
was nowhere near as bad as
thinking i would never be able to understand
or keep a hold of the meaning of a complete thought

my entire life had been
one great big experiment in values and ethics
reading
learning from life
quietly observing
thinking
translating life onto the page
and painting it's image on canvas

these expressions of what i had observed and learned
were the physical manisfestations
of the other part of the conversation
of my solitary life as an artist

depression

after the accident
except for the loud brain noise that never went away
my mind was empty
i had been shaken and all of the thoughts
and memories were
like these brightly colored ribbons
unraveled
cut away
without end and moving through
complete darkness

when i realized this loss
i grieved
no pill could make me better
and no pill could kill the pain either

i had good reason to be depressed
the memories of my children
and the life we shared were gone
the abilities to express life and thought
through art and writing were also gone
and i did not know if what i had spent years developing
would ever come back

i was no longer a strong person
who could do normal things
like go to a school function
without confusion and panic taking over
or go to a shopping mall
without walking all distorted

i was locked up inside

when i was out in public
normal people looked at me
and from far back in my eyes i watched them too
eating out in restaurants
strolling down sidewalks in town

depression

and then i started to notice
the invisible people
in wheelchairs
walking with canes
staring off quietly
going from one place to another
and without knowing how or when it happened
i realized
i had become an invisible person too
staring off and quietly going wherever
too slowly
trying to stay out of the way
trying to get there without being noticed
trying to look normal
something i am pretty sure
i never cared about back in the day
still
it bothered me
when people looked at me with sad eyes
or when people
not
looked at me
on purpose

for the first time i understood
the expression all of our invisible eyes shared
we were crying from way far back inside
do you see me
i am in here

after about two years i told my doctor
if i was depressed
i wanted to be depressed
and begin dealing with whatever was bothering me

i wanted off of the pills that made me
not feel anything

depression

after the doctor helped me get off the medication
i felt like i had been thrown
splash
into the reality of life
i was terrified i was losing my mind

what would happen if i let people know i needed help
would my children be taken away
these thoughts continued to haunt me

with a lot of help from my neuro-psyche dr. denman
and my local therapist dr. wong
i learned that life was easier to understand
when i faced my fears

deceiving myself and trying to make life fit
the way i wanted it to be
or pretending i was stronger than i really was
or believing other people
were something they were not
only made the acceptance and change i needed
to grow through
harder to attain

it was strange
even though i could not remember
the specifics of my life
the substance of all of those lessons
that were etched into my brain
were still there
strong and true

without knowing why
the core of who i had grown to be
had remained intact

the kids and i learned
over and over again that life was found in truth

depression

no matter how ugly or scary it was
the truth did make us free
and not looking at reality
well
was kind of a pointless waste of time

we learned that even though
the accident had stopped us for a while
we were able to help each other
move through the sadness toward recovery
by sharing our thoughts and flaws and life lessons
openly
we joined along side each other and
we grew
together

down the road

10. changes

for a long time
we lived through all of our life changes
without knowing what had caused them
and because of this the kids had to rely
on their own observations
and efforts at making sense out of
what had happened to all of us
without any help because
insurance did not cover any counseling for them
because well, it wasn't accident related

what was interesting was how they
adjusted to their own frustrations
especially during those first two years
of fog and confusion

that summer when matt came home
he noticed i slept most of the time
he missed me
his eyes were filled with so much love and concern
and helplessness
he was so young
only thirteen
and yet all he wanted to do was take care of us
he could not understand
why the doctors did not fix me
he was angry we were not getting the help we needed

at the end of the summer
when we took matt back to the airport
his eyes were filled with tears
and his face was flush with sadness and pain
he could not express
how much he wanted to stay
and i could not understand how
to help him

changes

steve was worried too
he was not prepared for how bad things were
he was so tender and sweet
and so young
just eleven years old
he could not understand what had happened to me
and i could not help him
because i did not understand what had happened either

that summer
a sadness appeared in his eyes
that had not been there before
and steve took to playing the guitar in his room

that first summer rebekah was a brave little soldier
afraid and not knowing where to turn to find safety
moving ever forward
quietly trying to understand what was happening
to her
to me
to all of us
she was still very much a young girl
who wanted to laugh and play with her friends

i remember once when i was in real bad shape
rebekah's eyes welled up with water
and she asked me
how do you live in so much pain
what keeps you from giving up
and i said
just now
when you told me about your day
that was the best moment of my life
i go through everything
for this one moment with you
listening to your voice
looking at your shining face

changes

and i am so grateful because
tonight
when i brought the covers up snug around your shoulders
and brushed the hair away from your eyes
all of the joy in my heart
told sorrow to wait just one minute

and when i whispered do you know why you have
freckles on your nose
it's because you are so sweet that while you are asleep
angels stop and give you little kisses
and that is why
when you wake up
you have tiny freckles on your nose

you see bekah
tonight
we were here
to give each other a good night hug
and a kiss on the cheek
we have enjoyed one more day together
and when i say sweet dreams pun'kin-pie
and turn out the light
and you chime back
sweet dreams mama
these moments
are my reason to live
these moments
are stronger than any pain

that night
when i gave bekah a kiss on her forehead
and we hugged and said good night to each other
i knew she understood
and i knew our connection would always be strong

steve showed his feelings in quiet ways
one day when i was in a lot of pain

changes

he came over and put his arm around me
his eyes were so sad when he looked at me

i hugged him
and patted him on the back
he held me to him and he said no mama
so i asked him what do you mean
and he said don't pat me on the back
when you do that you are saying good-bye

i could tell he was missing me
i told him *i am still in here*

his eyes filled with water
and he hugged me
and i whispered i love you too
and at that moment
our connection grew
beyond the strength of spoken words

matt's first thoughts were always
to protect us and keep us safe
he was fearless
he took it on himself to shield us from harm
with all of his heart and soul
all he wanted was to be with us
and even though he was too young
to be taking care of us
we were all comforted by his strength
and felt safe when he came back home to stay

during that time of our lives
there was a lot of chaos everywhere around us
making life harder than it needed to be

we did not have many good days to compare to the bad
we did not know why going outside
on a bright sunny day was too much for me
we did not know why

changes

it was harder for me to function outside
when the weather was bad
until later
after everything had already become too much for me
and by then my balance was so off
and the pain was so bad in my head
that all i could do was stare off and fall asleep

matt and steve became our comic relief
they loved funnin' and making us laugh
they teamed up as only brothers could
and climbed into hysterical characters they made up
while spinning outrageous tales
until we were laughing so hard we begged them to quit
which of course they never did
to this day when they get going
i know i will have to leave the room
if i am ever going to stop laughing
and to this day seeing me laugh
really makes them happy too

in the beginning of our changes
i was stubborn
i could have asked the kids to help me
but i wanted to take care of my own family
and i wanted my kids to know that i could
take care of them and our home

my problems doing this showed up in strange ways
when i washed the kitchen floor
it took me about two hours and it wore me out
why did it take so long
and why was it so hard to clean the floor
i had no idea

the house was usually empty and quiet
when i did my chores
i didn't want the kids to see how hard it was for me
i wanted everything to seem

changes

        normal
        even if it wasn't
        then one day matt noticed
        hey mom
        weren't you washing that same area
        when i left over an hour ago
        was i
        yeah i guess so
        matt kept checking on me
        through the rails of the stairway
        and that was how he figured out
        when i turned around and rinsed the mop out
        i forgot where i had just cleaned
        and kept walking back onto the wet floor
        making new messes all over again

        when he told me what i was doing
        i understood why it took nearly two hours
        to mop the kitchen floor
        matt figured out two tricks
        that helped me wash the floor
        first he put a little tag on the soap side of the bucket
        so i knew which side of the pale was soap suds
        and which side was my rinse water
        and then we decided it was best
        if i always started in the same corner of the room
        and ended by the stairs
        problem solved

        when i was out in the garden
        matt would tell me to come inside and take a break
        you have been outside too long ma
        his heart was so compassionate and so giving
        a lot of the time i felt like everything would be okay
        because matt was there
        we all did

        matt and steve and bekah were on a quest
        to figure out what made my brain shut down

changes

and how we could do things differently
to keep that from happening

they came up with the best practical ways
to help me on my way back to having an active life

the kids told me
they knew right when i was having a bad spell
they said they could see it in my eyes
my eyes got bigger and shiny
and my speech slurred

they figured out if kids
were running around in the house
i had a bad spell
if there was a lot of noise
i had a bad spell
it did not matter if it was laughter or loud talking
it did not matter if it was a happy day or i was tired
if there was a lot of movement around me
or a lot of noise or sudden noise
i had a bad spell
they saw when i was starting to have trouble
and they became the *don't run around mom* police

stephen became my confidant
he was always there to help
with the not so fun stuff
doing laundry or washing dishes
or helping with hard work outside
he figured out how to fix things
he understood love was more than saying i love you
love was practical
he always encouraged me to keep trying
he became fascinated with studies about
how the brain worked
and how memories were stored and recalled

steve noticed i had a better chance
of remembering more

changes

if my mind was already in an area of thought
if there was a direct link between
something that happened or was said and a memory
i might remember a portion of it
but if i was asked about the same memory directly
and we were not talking about it
and there was nothing else that stimulated the memory
then i remembered nothing

bekah realized that when i looked out of focus
she could put her hands on my face
and hold them there and talk to me
it helped

the kids also became very protective
sometimes they argued if either one of them
thought the other one made me tired
they would get angry with each other
they worried and did not want me to be tired
one day i told them
it was impossible for anyone to take advantage of me
because i willingly gave them everything i had
this had always been my life choice
to love them and
give them all of my heart with each new day
how they responded to that or what they did with that
was their life choice

giving to them did not make me tired
hearing them argue over who made me tired
was what wore me out
blaming someone because i had a bad spell
did not change anything
or make me all better
it wasn't anybody's fault
after that they stopped arguing
and grew even closer

changes

in the beginning
i was nervous i would embarrass the kids
by going to a school function
walking all wobbly with a cane
or leaving a program early
because i could not handle
all of the confusion anymore
but it turned out they were so happy i was there
that nothing else mattered

we realized our lives had forever changed
and we learned how to slow our pace
so we could all walk through life together

our connection grew so strong that we knew
no matter what happened
we were always going to love each other
and be there for each other

slowly
life moved us past our hard times
to the next birthday
and through the next season
until we found ourselves enjoying
those precious beautifully wrapped moments
of life once again

down the road

11. an independent purpose

it was so hard to work through
the feeling that i did not have
an independent purpose in life anymore
i had always loved to
work
and take care of my children

i looked forward to
finishing my book
painting my masterpiece
one day going back to college
getting my degree
teaching
and once the kids were busy with their own lives
i saw myself as an old silver haired lady
traveling to remote villages
and helping people

i did not realize how much this would all change
until one day
about a year after the accident
when we went to the lake to visit my sister
and her family at their summer home
which was around the bend
on a small lake in michigan
from where our grandparent's cottage was

the kids were having too much fun
being pulled behind the boat
on this huge yellow inflatable banana

at first they were squealing with laughter
then coming around the last curve toward home
something happened
the float that was never supposed to tip over
sent them flying into
the icy spring waters of the lake

an independent purpose

the kids were wearing life jackets
the older children helped the grownups
right the boat and get the younger ones
back to safety

but all i could do was stand there
and watch from the shore
and listen to the panic in their voices
and know that even if they were drowning
i could not swim out to save them

it all worked out all right
no one needed me
everything was okay

only it wasn't

i realized i could no longer protect or save my children
and if they ever needed me
i could not be counted on
to take care of my sister's children either
and i stood there alone
trying to focus through the tears

it was a shock
realizing i could not be depended upon
realizing i needed to depend on others
sometimes even my children

all of my life i had worked so hard
to be independent and free
suddenly i could do nothing
to make life secure for my family
i had to rely on other people's opinions
of my condition to get the care i needed
i had to rely on other people doing the right thing
in order for us to survive as a family
it was the worst kind of
helplessness

an independent purpose

through years of rehab
i learned how to take care of my family
and myself again
i learned how to use planners
and calendars and files and make lists
so i could set goals and achieve them
and find my way back
to living
with an independent
purpose

12. a new life

after a few years of out patient therapies
and a divorce
the kids and i moved to our small farm
in michigan
where it was quiet
and we could listen to the wind blow
and the morning doves coo

we enjoyed the simple pleasures of life
like having fires in the fire pit
and watching the stars
as they appeared through the lavender twilight
after a beautiful big sky sunset
it was perfect
country

at our crossroads
the good ol' boys still waited for a woman to go first
even if she did drive up to the stop sign after he did
and people were not in a hurry
unless there really was a fire

the kids made terrific friends at school
and we had great neighbors

we had found paradise
on wayne and linda's front porch
at big eric's backyard venison bar-b-ques
on jill and doug's deck tippin' a bell's brew
where we learned about mules and donkeys
over at jeff and anna's watchin' the kids grow
and in bill and laura's barn
where we learned about horses

over the years jill
the trouble maker
became my best friend

a new life

she'd show up in my driveway with her truck
and holler let's go woman
get your butt in gear
and we'd go to an art show or a forest preserve
or garage sales
she took me around to the local spots
where i met the sweetest bunch of people
i could ever hope to know
and she even got me to go camping
which was something i used to really enjoy

because of her encouragement and persistence
i developed the confidence i needed
to get on with living again
so thanks jilleeee

our neighbors and my kids and their friends
were so kind
they didn't care if i walked all wobbly
they liked my gentleness and valued me as a person
and i loved them all right back

when the weather was nice
and someone had a fire going
it was an open invitation
for anybody to stop by and visit
we had so much fun razzing each other
in the summer we had spontaneous tractor meets
in the winter eric plowed us out after a snow storm
and when the mules or horses or our llamas got loose
we had all kinds of fun rounding them up

someone at rehab had suggested
that i buy a llama for the farm
okay i thought
sounds good
i have always loved animals
so we bought the sweetest young male you ever saw
then we bought a young pregnant female for him

a new life

so they would get along and he would not be lonely
and naturally the llamas grew in numbers

they liked coming in the house in the summer time
and sniffing my freshly perked coffee
and i got a kick out of watching them
resting with them in the shade of a wide reaching tree
out in the pasture
and going for walks with them
they were easier for me to handle
than a dog on a leash
and they were the best landscaping team
and home security system i would ever need

seeing the llamas through my window in the morning
gave me a reason to get up
i would put the coffee on and get dressed
and after a cupper
i'd go out to check on the animals
and make sure they had grain and hay and water
those chores started my day and helped nudge me on
to the next thing i needed to do
until the day was done

up until the time we bought our llamas
i had worried about getting depressed
once the kids were on their own
i was afraid i would go from one lost day
to the next without doing anything useful

i was worried the kids
might not follow their own paths
if they thought i needed them to take care of me
so the llamas were my first step toward
building a fulfilling independent life
they were easy to take care of and very gentle
and funny and
definitely one of the best decisions i ever made

a new life

jill made sure we had plenty of cats for our barns
and thanks to jeff's parents we had a precious akita
we also had a dainty flower of an english bulldog
a maltese who was the boss and
a german shepherd mix we got from the humane society
who was a great herding dog
and they all made sure none of the big animals
stepped on the mama
we bought a mule for bekah to ride
a burro to keep the mule in the pasture
and miniature donkeys because they were too cute
oh and we got a pigmy goat
to eat the burdock
isn't that right mike

countless good friends
helped us when we were mending fences
catching loose llamas
and even house sat
when we went to visit my sister
or went camping for a few days
thank you dana-dooo

we kept our rubber boots and a staff by the door
we wore overalls and flannel shirts
we loved going to the quality farm and fleet
we learned the difference between
a first and second cutting of hay
and our most used tools were
wire cutters and hammers and a pitch fork

we had our own organic garden
and lived frugally
i had been a hard worker all of my life
whether i worked in an office
or was up a ladder painting a building
writing or drawing or painting a canvas

a new life

i was always working
so farm life was a perfect fit
there was always something that needed doing
fences to tighten
weeds to pull
trees to prune
seeds to plant
and crops to harvest
and i could do these things
at my own pace

we had six acres of good organic hay pastures
and a farmer who lived nearby
baled our hay
and then took away what we didn't need
in exchange for filling our barn in the summer

our ten acres
had become a thriving community
of two legged and four legged
pack animals
staying in one place

it had been a long time since
i felt safe
and it was
all
good

13. reading

reading had always been
an important part of my life
in fact i did not mind being alone
as long as i could read

but after the accident
when i tried to read
it wore me out
i could see alright
but everything looked different
words in a book floated all over the page
and looked like shades of gray
and black symbols
circles and half circles and wavy lines
that did not make any sense
similar letters in a word or sentence
next to each other
were hard to tell apart
it took so much concentration
and left me in so much pain and drained
that i did not even want to try to read
why bother when whatever i read
did not make any sense
and was forgotten anyway

reading which had been such a pleasure
had become close to impossible
filling out forms was too complicated
and i could no longer make sense
out of abstract ideas or symbolism
and when i did understand something i read
it was a great moment
but then it just disappeared with the next distraction
lost forever in that
i haven't gotta clue place in my brain

reading

there were long periods of time
when i stopped trying to read
it was too frustrating to struggle with something
i had always loved to do
it reminded me of all that i wasn't anymore
and it made me sad

the people at rehab helped me want to keep trying
they helped me use a card marker
the card had a line of paper cut out
that left me with just enough room
to read one line at a time
i learned how to mark off what i had read
so i would not keep reading the same pages
over and over again

i found out that if i took a break
after reading one thought or scene
and then picked up the book again later
and read less and read slower
i could follow a storyline

i had always loved to learn
it never mattered how thick a book was
or how long it took to read
i enjoyed going right to the source of a teaching
because i liked deciding for myself
what i thought about other people's ideas
the funny thing about my memory was that
the impressions of what i had learned stayed with me
what changed
was that i could not remember what books i had read
or who the authors were
or the details to back up
what i knew about their teachings

i used to pick up a book
nobody in particular
and anonymously merge

reading

into another consciousness
i enjoyed discovering great thinkers
traveling through time to other places
and exploring historical lessons

judging by their worn pages
the people who influenced me the most were
henry david thoreau   ralph waldo emerson
viktor e. frankl   albert einstein
robert frost   lao tsu and shakespeare
even though i could not pull specifics
about their work from my mind
to explain the affects their writings had on my life
their substance
had worked their way through my own character

i went to the library
and told the nice people there
about my problem with memory
and described how words were all over a page
and how i did not remember what i just read
i made a list of who and what i liked to read
from my many books at home
and shared how much i wanted to keep reading
and those precious ladies
helped me find short simple stories
and large print books
and my kids helped too
they recommended books they had enjoyed
when i read them their bed time stories
those books were a great beginning
and i was so happy to be reading again

i found out if a book only had two main characters
i could understand it okay
and even though i still did not remember much
i saw moving pictures in my mind when i read

reading

and that was so exciting
a few minutes every day i experienced
imagination
and one more piece of my life was returning

back when i was in rehab
someone figured out that the littlest distraction
like yawning or looking away from a book
or hearing something
was all it took to make me lose my place
or lose track of the story
and any thought that went with it
and even though that never got any better
i did learn how to work around that problem
at first i read a line or paragraph and then
went on to reading a page or two
before i went to sleep
or when the house was quiet

it did not matter if i was tired and
could only read a couple of lines
or a couple of pages
i was reading
i felt free again
to learn
and to imagine
and that was
well
wonderful

14. music

that first year all music sounded like
too much
confusing noise
that did not make any sense
when the radio was on
i could not recognize who was singing
i could not make out the words being sung
or figure out what the song was about
there wasn't any connection between the music
and my life
it was all too weird

since the sixties i had lived and breathed music
and loved it all
playing classical piano had been a major part of my life
music composition and orchestration
was my second major in college back then
and yet after the accident when i heard music
all i wanted was quiet
abstract had become too hard to hold onto
i think because it was where i lived

one day i went to a store with the kids
and recognized a cd cover
it was joni mitchell
i bought it
suddenly i was listening to something familiar

i found a great music store in kzoo
called the flipside
it was small enough to handle
which was way cool
the only problem was i got lost
every time i tried to find the place
and i'm talkin' this happened for years people
oh and there was one more little problem
once i did find it

music

park and go inside
seeing all of that stuff on the shelves
and on the walls left me feeling woozy
and blank and
without any freakin' idea what i went there to buy
after going there for a year and not buying much
i called the owner to see if we could find a way
to get around this difficulty
we laughed about how much
we didn't remember of the sixties and
when i told neal i had a certifiable reason
we laughed some more

over the phone neal and doc
figured out from the smallest clue
who played the music i liked and what cd it was on
and then they ordered or set aside the cd for me
so when i got to the store to pick it up
the cd was behind the counter with my name on it
those guys did more than sell me a cd
they helped bring back an important part of my life
music and the love of music
thanks neal - thanks doc

i was listening to music again
with great pleasure i found my old faves
bob dylan   the beatles   the moody blues
pink floyd and the eagles and the doors
james taylor   simon and garfunkel   fleetwood mac
leo kotke   taj mahal   the allman brothers
janis joplin and the james gang
jimi hendrix   ravi shankar   john mayall
leon russell   stevie ray vaughan and stevie wonder
my old friends even gave me some relief
from the constant buzzing and ringing noise
inside my head

for quite a while after the accident
i preferred listening to country music

music

i think it was because it was different
from what i used to listen to
when the radio was on a country station
i wasn't thinking i should remember this song
i wasn't reminded of how much i had lost
it was all new

i loved willie nelson and patsy cline
and i really dug the new talent
shania twain   the dixie chicks and martina mcbride
it was great listening to spunky women
who sang about living free of abuse
and who took a hold of their dreams and
worked hard to make them a reality

i also loved listening to tim mcgraw
hello
and alan jackson
what a sweetie-pie
the way those guys sang about country life
and how they loved their wives through their music
was the bees knees

i had finally accepted
that i could not keep track of everything
and it didn't matter anymore if i knew
what the words were in a song
or who was singing
or what the name of the song was
i was groovin' again and that
was the point

i found my way back to
duke ellington and louis armstrong
to etta james and nancy wilson and nat king cole
to frank sinatra and barbra streisand and tony bennett
and then i got to cookin' and took the col'trane
to a love supreme and felt jazzed all over again
from the inside out

music

i discovered that music helped me
on a few really important levels
playing a little enya or the secret garden
or celtic music at night set on a low volume
seemed to relieve the loud noise in my head
i didn't feel like banging my head into the wall as often
and this helped me fall asleep easier

during the warm months
when i worked on oil paintings
music helped me concentrate
on what i was expressing on the canvas

when i painted the embrace i listened to
alanis morissette and sarah mclachlan
the david matthews band and
the city of angels soundtrack and aaliyah
when i worked on celebration
i listened to brazilian salsa and neal young
tito and tarantula and los lobos
and the desperado soundtrack
and when i worked on the journey series
i listened to the soundtracks of
schindler's list and the city of angels
and to itzhak perlman   moby
robbie robertson   tool and mozart

any music that had substance
honesty
direction
and passion
inspired me

when i put on those ear phones
the world slipped away
and for a little while i was focused
and i felt like maybe i wasn't such a
stranger in a strange land after all

15. writing

after the accident my writing was all messed up
my spelling was terrible
and it was impossible to organize my thoughts

i had always loved the written word
and thanks to my grandmother reading to me
from a very young age
i could recite robert frost and shakespeare
before i could write

expressing myself through the written word
came as naturally to me as breathing
i had studied at columbia college in chicago
in the early seventies and for many years
worked very hard to develop my skills
and then suddenly
my abilities were gone

i had been working on a book
based on interviews i had conducted with people
who were holocaust survivors
and world war two veterans
i had been working on this project
for about five years
it was nearly finished
when the crash happened

at some point i tried to get on the computer
to work on the book
but i froze the thing up
i couldn't handle looking at the screen
or figure out how to find my book
every time i tried
i failed
i remembered that i had felt so lucky
to have met the people

writing

whose stories i had written
when i looked at the portraits i had done of them
their eyes were filled with so much pain and sorrow
and hope and wisdom

for many years i had searched for understanding
i wanted to know how people
ordinary people
could justify killing others
or hurting anyone
because of a belief
a philosophy
a religion
a political point of view
or for the sake of some personal advantage

i did not understand how some people
could have ignored and then justified
what happened during the second world war
and i wondered
what had become of humanity
where was god
was god ever on the side of war and killing
was god moved to intervene when
the innocent were plucked from the earth
and stacked in piles to burn like unwanted weeds

for years i quietly hoped
to find answers
while i interviewed these incredible people
and wrote their life stories

after the accident
i could not listen to the tapes of the interviews
or read the hard copy
with corrections scribbled on their worn pages
i could not hold onto thoughts long enough
to work on or finish the book

writing

and sitting at the computer screen for ten minutes
gave me so much head pain
that i had to give up

a deep sorrow filled my heart
and i grieved

i should have made better use of my time
i should have worked faster
i had been careless with the one thing
these people had learned long ago
never take for granted
today or tomorrow

after we moved to the farm
and my life quieted down
i decided to stop giving up
and i started writing again
it began slowly
we got this little computer and the internet
josh wrote down detailed instructions
and helped me get to a philosophy chat room
and i found that when someone else
started the conversation
it helped me get those writing juices flowing

an old friend and i found each other on the internet
and as we caught up with what had been going on in life
something really cool happened
thoughts flowed through my fingers
one line at a time
almost like
poetry

after the accident i always felt like
i might not live long enough
to share with my children how much i loved them
and how precious life was

writing

i wanted to make sure that when they were older
they would know this
i wanted to write my thoughts down
but i couldn't express myself with the same ease
i used to feel writing anymore

and then i thought
so what if i can't keep track of sentence structure
i would write without sentences
paragraphs or punctuation
the work had its own natural flow
the computer fixed my spelling errors
searches helped me find repeated phrases
and copying and pasting made moving things around
into some kind of order that made sense
much easier when i was editing
and it had a great thesaurus
which was a huge help because
at first most of the words i used were one syllable

the more i wrote
the more i discovered there was still
one part to writing i had in my heart
the substance of the story

more of my life was being restored
if ten minutes of writing was all i could handle
that was how long i wrote
ten minutes here and there
added up to a lot of work over two years time
which was how long it took me
to write this little book

i learned how to use medical reports
calendars and journals
for the details of life i had lost
and when i needed more information than that
i asked the children what they remembered

writing

there was a way back to expressing myself
through the written word
and i had found it

the longing i had
to feel the connection with people i did not know
through writing
or to share moments of revelation
with people i would never meet
was being fulfilled

what anyone else thought about my writings
did not matter
i was writing again
i was recording what i saw
and what i lived through
and that was all i ever really wanted to do anyway

i was expressing what was in my heart
and as long as i did not try to think about it first
there with all candor
for you and me to discover at the same time
was an uncapitalized
genuine picture of life
written
one line at a time

16. painting

before the accident
i was working on
what i thought was the last painting in the series
called the faces of a woman

i used to love to think about
everything
what i was going to paint
what the message would be
which brush to use
color and form and well everything
i looked at the sky
and thought about color and light
i was always observing nature and learning
holding images in my memory
to brush out later on canvas

being an artist was
like being life's sponge
i soaked up experiences and
absorbed observations
and when i was full
a tangible form of expression was released
on paper or canvas

after the accident i looked at a canvas and thought
nothing
i picked up a brush and took some color
and put it somewhere
no inspiring life lessons came to mind
the fire was gone
and i was a cold empty cave

when i did try to paint
things that used to be easy
like deciding which colors to use
or finding the colors i needed in my paint box

painting

had become impossible
seeing all of those tubes of color in my case
confused me
what did i just want to put on the canvas
i didn't know

when i dug through my paints long enough
i found the color i needed
but until i saw it there was nothing but
blackness

after a short time i was exhausted
the pain in my head
was so intense i could not function
i had to stop
when i finished the painting
grieving
i did give up for awhile
and then lynne at rehab and dr denman
helped me understand that
even though i did not have
the emotions or memories to urge me on
i could paint
all i had learned before the accident
was still in my brain somewhere
all i had to do was work
and art would once again find its way out

and then it happened
i stopped worrying about the process
and painted
whatever i thought or felt was expressed
one brush stroke at a time
i set a separate tray out on the table
for the oils i was using
and put colors
in the order they where placed on my palette
i let go of any expectations and just created
for however long my concentration lasted

painting

i had always hoped that
people who saw my work
would feel and connect with
something true in it
that they would know they were not alone

i realized that if the only people
to see and feel my work
were my family and friends
it was okay
i did not need to sell any of my paintings
what really mattered was the work
the process of creation
that was my reward

when i painted
my ideas about
the meaning of life
the people i had known
and all of my experiences and feelings
were fused together

hope returned and i thought
maybe the people i had interviewed
would be honored in this way one day
through my artwork

and so i continued to paint
without a plan
because i had a purpose
and a journey to share

17. my senses

the doctors explained to me that my senses
were not communicating like before
ok
what did that mean
we had no way of understanding
how many areas of life
that would affect
usually the kids figured it out
backwards
they thought about what was going on
right before i started feeling out of it
and then tried to figure out
what senses were overloaded

we discovered that if there was a shadow
or it was suddenly dark
i lost all sense of space and depth
if it was windy or raining or snowing
i became disoriented
and might fall down like a leaf

for a long time i did not like going outside
even though i missed being in the weather
or going to an art exhibit in the park
or making a snowman with the kids after a storm
because everything felt so foreign to me out there

in time we learned i could enjoy going outside
or being around people more
when i wore ear plugs and special glasses
and took a cane along for balance

in quiet unpressured situations
i communicated better
if too much was going on
then my mind followed

my senses

whatever was happening around me visually
i wasn't able to concentrate or stay focused
or block out background noises
the more conflict and activity
the slower my senses were interpreted in my brain
and i started to stutter or my speech slurred
or i drifted off to a quiet place
my balance getting so bad i looked drunk
without ever touching a drop of alcohol

my eyes not scanning and my brain injury
effected my ability to drive too
when i tried to drive
at night on the highway
it looked like i was traveling at warp speed
in a sci-fi movie
with these long shooting lines of colored light
disappearing into deep space

out of the darkness
split second
close ups
of trees
or maybe a truck in the next lane
appeared
fully formed out of the confusion

clearly
i saw some thing
my heart was pounding
as i told myself to stay calm
go slow
breathe in
breathe out
don't scream

and then i just wanted to go home
away from any road

my senses

to where it was safe and still

over time we learned what i could
and could not do

we did not stop going to restaurants
we went to restaurants that were cozy
when they weren't busy
i gave up going to indoor concerts
even small ones
every time i went to one
i only lasted fifteen or twenty minutes
before i felt too disoriented to stay
we have gone to a couple of outdoor events
if there was a place where i could sit
that was quiet
and if i could paint or color with oil crayons
i could almost handle the event
though i paid for it later with terrible bad head pain
and was wiped out for a few days

every once in a while
something neat like the lilith fair came along
and the dixie chicks and queen latifah
were going to be there
and we just had to go
my son steve bought us tickets
and arranged for a ride with friends
and problems or no
we went to the concert
and we had a great time

i didn't have to stop enjoying life
even if it did mean i was going to suffer later
and we didn't have to stop going places in the car
even though the days of taking off and traveling
on cross country road trips
with the radio up and the windows down

my senses

were over
and going anywhere at night
wasn't happening anymore with ease either
a few miles to the grocery or to school and back home
was about all i could handle

it took a lot of detective work
before we figured some things out
we found if i drove short distances
and stayed in the slow lanes
and i kept my eyes
on the tail lights of the car in front of me
and drove mostly in the day time
before the roads were crowded
i did okay

when the weather was bad
i stayed home and took it easy
and remembered the point of my trip
wasn't only about getting there
it was also about
being here

18. the movies

another step toward getting my life back
was going to the movies
i had studied film in college
and always loved going to the movies

something came out we wanted to see
it might have been michael starring john travolta
we decided it was time to give it a try
arm in arm the kids and i
walked through the dim theater
i held my head up and tried to look normal
but my feet gave me away
as they clomped down
in search of the floor

we found a seat
good
i got through that
breathe
and then the theater grew dark
and the movie began
it was great
until the movie was over and i tried to walk
my body was all over the place
and when we went out
into the light of the complex
my eyes slammed shut
it was too bright
panic
i couldn't see
i froze
the kids found a quiet place for me to sit
and relax for a few minutes
until i could walk better

the movies

over the next few years
we tried different movies
we found out that movies with special effects
and bright lights going on and off
gave me a really bad spell
we found that
if the camera moved around real fast
i got dizzy
and if the plot was complicated i got lost
we learned if i kept my special glasses on
and put in my ear plugs
and if we waited until the theater cleared out
and the lights went back on
i could handle leaving the theater a little better
though nothing helped my walking
my sense of balance
was pretty much gone after seeing a movie
no matter what we did i was wobbly

i learned i did not have to give everything up
usually movies with special effects
and complicated plots
i watched at home
where i was free to pause and review
anything that seemed to move too fast
for some reason the smaller screen of the tv
wasn't as hard on my brain to process

because of my memory problems
when we went to a movie rental store
i never knew which films i had already seen
but once i started watching one
if i had seen the movie before
it would feel familiar
but the only thing i remembered
was how it made me feel
a strong impression about the movie remained
but that was it

the movies

i could see a movie over and over
and it was like seeing it for the first time
every time
which my kids have always found
extremely entertaining

i did go see the new star wars movie
when it was in the theater
man i was all ready for a terrible reaction
i had a back up plan
it was simple
easy to remember
leave as soon as you feel woozy
only it never happened
i wondered why
it turns out the movie had been filmed
a new digital way
and something about this new way
made a difference
i did not feel sick at the end of the movie

about four years after the accident
a movie came out i really wanted to see
it was called the horse whisperer
for some reason i wound up going to that one alone
it was so painful to watch that i sobbed out loud
many times
when the movie was over
i was so shaken that i could not move
by the time i did get up to leave
the theater was empty
my body felt like rubber
my feet clomped as they tried to find the floor
the cane was my helper
going up the incline to the exit
the bright light in the big room
made my eyes go open and shut
it was hard to see
i was a twisted walking mess

the movies

i kept going
people were looking at me
i kept going wishing i was normal again

when i got out to the car
i couldn't stop crying
what was happening to me
was i having a breakdown
what was so upsetting about that movie

i started seeing a shrink around that time
he was a wonderful human being with a kind heart
and he was easy to talk with
he helped me have confidence in my reason
and accept that even though life was different
it still could make sense

in the beginning we talked about the accident
and how life had changed
sometimes we talked about the movie
the horse whisperer
i was determined to figure out why
i had such a strong reaction to that movie
i decided to read the book no matter how long it took
which was good because it took a long time
i even went back to see my neuro-psych
because i was worried
that movie had triggered something
i had become weepy
especially when i was alone

dr. denman explained that my emotional processing
had slowed down too
so when something real intense happened
i experienced a rush of feelings
and even though there was a reason why i had them
memory loss and the brain injury
had obscured my ability
to process these more complex abstract ideas

the movies

by the time the movie ended in the theater
i had no idea what scenes made me cry
i just knew i had been moved to the core

once the horse whisperer came out on video
i watched it over and over again
and took notes
sorting through the story
and the tears that would always come
with the help of dr. denman i realized
i was relating to the injured horse
all of the fear and pain
and loss of trust in humanity
that horse felt
had also filled my heart

the humanity and patience of the horse trainer
had shocked me into realizing
that there was a part of me
that felt isolated by being different now
somehow i knew
that there would probably never be anyone
who would wait out in a field for me
i was scarred
and this broke my heart

later i faced every emotion
and every painful truth
and then
i got over it
and got on with living
and as it turns out
i am wonderfully loved by a few amazing people
who have told me and shown me
they would wait anywhere for me for forever

19. a romantic lead

i doubted if there would ever be
another man who would laugh at my jokes
and get a kick out of my quirks
and after the divorce
i asked myself
would i even be able to trust anyone anyway
or give of myself with my whole heart
again

it was strange getting used to the idea that at forty
i might never have another lover
i thought about life and how we never know
when we would share our lives with a companion
or make love
for the last time

i did not have the confidence in my ability
to know the difference between
a man who was sincere and kind
and one who would
manipulate me into a life of quiet desperation

when i put on weight
it was almost a relief
dealing with someone not looking at me
because i was heavy
was somehow easier than
feeling unattractive
because i was damaged goods

it took some time before i understood that
getting all stirred up and trying to
define what love was and
who it would come from
was just plain silly

a romantic lead

my family and friends loved me
my dingbat animals loved me
and i loved them all right back
life was good and i was grateful
i realized my life was filled with love

my need to hold onto domestic turmoil
just to hear those words
i love you so much i can't live without you
had been resolved
and so i embraced the comfort of my solitude

i was creatively productive
and felt a connection with all of life
i did not need one person
for a sense of validation

and that was when
life
became the object
of my affection

20. teaching my children well

there was a time in my life
when i was certain
i would always have the health and strength
to take care of my children
i knew they would always be able to depend on me
the thought never came into my mind for a second
that i might need to rely on them
when they were still so young

all i had ever wanted was to give my children
time to grow up
to enjoy the carefree days of youth
and keep watch as they slept gently through the night
the idea that they might go through all of those days
without me
was paralyzing

an urgency filled my every thought
it shook me out of the loss i felt
when facing my limitations
and gave me the stamina to go on
i could not leave my children unprepared

i began to ask myself tough questions
what had been the greatest obstacles in my life
what had i learned from them
what had i taught my children
had the example i set for them been
good enough
had i
taught my children well enough
would they grow up to be humane people
would they be able to protect themselves
from those who would hurt them

teaching my children well

would they be able to think for themselves
when they needed to sort out
what their motivations were
or when they had to ask and answer
their own questions

would they be able to appreciate every challenge
every awakening
every stumble
when they were still so
not ready to be in this world on their own
i worried about who would love them if i died
not that i was so great
it was just that all their lives
they had been raised with love and respect
they knew i cared about every thought
and every feeling they had

i didn't have the luxury of missing one opportunity
to share an insight or life lesson with them
or worry about what would happen to them if i died
life had too many truly important things to focus on
to waste

as they grew older
a sense of familiarity would often arise
from what they were going through
and i would find myself
walking down the aisles of a library or a bookstore
where i would rediscover old friends from long ago
who had opened my mind to new ways of thinking
and in time they read the books
i had left on the tabletops
and as they expressed their thoughts and perceptions
their joys and frustrations
i in turn shared mine
and together we grew
some times i was their teacher
and some times they were mine

down the road

21. the thought

i realized
no one had all of the answers
and anyone who claimed otherwise
was crafting their own version of reality

being smart meant nothing
if it did not lead
a greater ability to give of ourselves
graciously

all the good and appreciating life stuff
came from the heart
one unselfish act at a time

and no matter how agonizing our growth was
and regardless of our mistakes and ignorance
the best thoughts we could have were these

when i had the opportunity to give
did i
did i appreciate the beauty of this moment

when i made the choice to respect others
whether or not they respected me
was i content in knowing that
this way of honoring all of life
some how enhanced
the connections i shared while living it

had i let go of the need to define
some absolute truth

i had always been a flower child
the ideals of living in harmony
with people and nature

the thought

had always been the central focus
of my thoughts

most of my life
i was mindful of the way i treated others
i tried not to say hurtful things
or make careless decisions that caused others pain
looking always to the heart of an issue
and figuring out what was troubling me
and then working on changing
my attitudes and perceptions
rather than wasting time judging others
and creating elaborate alibis
for my own self-centeredness

i had come to believe that life was about
a journey toward a clarity of thought
not perfection

and even though i had tried real hard not too
i had also stumbled down the
idiot pit a time or two just like everybody else

these ideals combined with practical life choices
opened my mind to
new ways of understanding
we were not all born to look and act the same
we were not all born with the same abilities
we were not all born tall or blonde
or rich or strong

we *were* all born
unique

we did not need to be strong to reach out
and give a hand to someone in need
we did not need to be tall to show empathy
and give someone a shoulder to cry on

the thought

we did not need to be smart
to love someone from a sick bed
or show compassion when
others were suffering heartache
we could even be simple minded
and weak and frail
and still we could give back
with gratitude
to nature and to humanity

the awareness of this connection
transcended every reason for
exclusion and indifference and
alienation and insecurity
because we were all an extension of each other

the way we choose to live
for all of us
had the potential to be
a wonderful creative expression
because the contribution we made
was realized
not solely by what we accomplished
but most importantly by the way we lived

being with people who value what we share
who understand that free love
means to love freely
has always been a special treat
and for a long time i believed
everyone was kind and principled
but that wasn't reality either

we often collide with others who like us
struggle between selfishness and charity
and who like us
wrestle with truths we do not want to face
often tripping over the obstacles we have created

the thought

i have learned how to be okay
with seeing life the way it is
often from more than one perspective at a time
and have stopped trying to convince myself
that life was the way i thought it should be

it was a tremendous challenge
to learn how to protect myself from
harmful misconceptions
self-destructive behaviors
and deceptive people

having the confidence to step out
into new ways of thinking and being
turned out to be a constant source of enrichment
in my life

and thoughts that once caused me to ponder
what is reality
does anyone really know what time it is
what is freedom
and if not now
when
had given way to these
reality is everything and it is always changing
time is continual
we are all connected to all of it

regardless of what is going on around us
freedom is found within

and now is all we have

this fleeting moment to be

and this fleeting moment to become

22. the lesson

my decisions and life choices
did not depend on whether i was
understood or respected or
appreciated or even loved in return

nothing
not even memory loss
could erase one bit of the self-centered life
i had sacrificed
while becoming a humane person

even if i did not remember the particulars
the impressions that had been
scorched into my character
were permanent
i did not have to remember the events in my life
that had caused me to grow and make decisions
differently
i did not have to remember
the times i had chosen to treat others with a respect
they had not shown me
those life lessons
had determined who i was a long time ago

it took time and a lot of help
before i could set boundaries
with the few people i knew
who seemed to enjoy living in chaos
and the misery it created

rationalizing why people did what they did
and trying to figure out what people really meant
had become impossible to keep track of
and besides all of that confusion
gave me really bad head pain

the lesson

so i figured
if there were people in my life who did not care
about the pain they were causing me
then maybe it was time for me
to stop the pain
face my fears
and leave the soap opera behind

i started paying attention to what people did
since excuses and reasons
were just too complicated to understand
and well
actions reflected what the truth really was anyway

i had seen for myself
that some one could look me right in the eye
cry
express undying love
and claim with incredible sincerity that
they would never do anything to hurt me
and lie

wow
talk about a moment of truth
i did not know people could do that
but some can

and that was when i realized
giving everyone the benefit of the doubt
was delusional
i had to face the truth
i had to stop waiting to be saved or fixed
i had to make sure i was not going to be a victim
and i had to let go of the few people
who had been hurting me

i learned the hard way
that there were people out there
who did exactly what they wanted to do

the lesson

no matter who it hurt
and who seemed to be okay with
spending the rest of their lives stumbling over
the clever reasons they had invented
so they could disguise their own cruelty
and appear as though
they had never done anything wrong
wearing all of those rationalized rights and wrongs
like shiny cubic zirconia rings on their fingers and toes

my balance came
when i learned through the pain
that i did not have to let people
walk all over me and hurt me
to be truly giving or loving
sometimes saying no
was exactly the most honest and
honorable thing to do for everyone

the truth was i had changed
i wasn't little and young or quick like i had been before
i had aged twenty years overnight and was slow
so what
i was able to give my family love today
and i was determined
to appreciate this gift of life
and never carelessly throw it away

besides the kids thought i was a cutie
whether i walked with a cane or not

the most important lessons i learned through it all
where these
give up the least amount possible
work on everything
never quit quitting
never stop starting
never give up
work and work until you find a way
to move forward

the lesson

and always remember
and never forget

give up the least amount possible

when you hear you can't do it
keep trying
when you feel you will never meet your goal
keep trying
slow and steady wins the race
what difference does it make
how long it takes you to overcome a problem
some difficulties take years to work through

don't be afraid to change
accept life the way it is
and then appreciate every bit of it

and don't beat yourself up if you fail
keep trying
because sometimes failure is
the fuel
that accelerates us
to go further down the road
than we ever thought was possible

23. acceptance

accepting life as it was took time
if i accepted my limitations it meant
i had them
and that was a hard pill to swallow

even though
everything i tried to do
especially those first two years
reminded me of my limitations
i fought
accepting them
until
pain and failure taught me
it was better
to go on with life
whatever that meant
than
to go
nowhere
in denial

once i accepted
life had changed
i adjusted to the way it was
and found peace and comfort
in each wonder-filled day

and that was when every ability i lost
and every memory i had forgotten
was never missed again

24. spirituality

i couldn't keep track of holidays
i couldn't drive to religious organizations
or support groups
i couldn't afford to go to yoga classes

whatever it was that used to ignite a spark
and get me going
was stuck in neutral

still i had a longing to
make sense of this human experience

despite the vulnerability and trauma
i needed to find a reason why this happened
so i could feel safe again

questions that i had grappled with most of my life
became even more important to answer
was there a god
was god the answer
to those life experiences we could not understand

or had the traditions and myths
passed down from one generation to the next
been created out of our own need to
sleep gently through the night

was there a god who intervened on our behalf
when we prayed was anyone listening

when bad things happened
was this because we had not lived up to
an impossible standard of perfection
that we had created ourselves

was it possible for the created thing
to describe it's creator

spirituality

could we ever understand our own purpose
the purpose of all of creation
or god's purpose

should we really assume that our intelligence
was the absolute epicenter of existence

after all
hadn't our ancestors once believed
the world was flat
because they couldn't imagine
what lay beyond the distant horizon

hadn't people once believed that
all of the planets and stars and galaxies
revolved around the earth

hadn't people on every continent
set aside a place that inspired them
and called it sacred ground

was it possible that our view
of god and spirituality
was so egocentric
that we couldn't see the sheer beauty
of our existence
without the conditions we had placed there

when people said to me
it was god's will that you survived
was that true
was that really true
what about the hard working father
who was driving the car that came into our lane
who died in the crash
was it god's will that he die
was it god's will
that he left behind a widow and three children

spirituality

if that was true
what made my life so special
i was a single mom
i had accomplished nothing
i loved my family but so did he
i had three children to care for
but so did he
no
something about that way of thinking
did not feel right

why would god cause such suffering
was god spiteful
was i that bad that not only i was being punished
but also an innocent man and his family
had been stricken as well
no
that did not feel right either

i kept thinking about a couple i knew
who years earlier had lost their baby daughter
to an illness
and how devastated they were
when their perceived lack of faith
had failed their precious little angel

i kept seeing the faces of holy people
who were filled with hatred
for those who believed differently
and i couldn't get past
all of the exclusionary clauses
and the wars and cruelty that had been fought
to defend and perpetuate them

the source of the wisdom of our ancestors
and the traditions that we cherished
were precious

spirituality

but had our need to preserve these truths
that were passed down to us
blinded us from seeing it

i began to wonder if we were all a little right
and a little wrong about how we defined
this eden

all of these questions overwhelmed me
and then one day i sat on the ground
and poured out my heart to a god who
may or may not be there
who may or may not listen
and who may or may not exist
the way i had imagined
and accepted
that those things didn't matter to me anymore
because i appreciated every element of this life
for the sake of it's fragility and magnificence

and that was when my prayer simply became
thank you
i found peace within and throughout the
connection

the mysteries that had plagued me so long
and the injustices that used to keep me up at night
no longer stopped me from
living fully engaged
in this amazing life worth living

25. the reward

the reward in all of this tragedy
was having learned how to appreciate
everything

hard lessons have taught me
to be patient
my awareness of life was
after all
relative

it turns out my ability to understand
the meaning of life
was not a necessary element
for it's continuation
which was pretty cool
i was a part of the expression
of our contemporary evolution
not the center of the universe
and i could live with that

i let myself off the hook
relaxed
and choose to accept life as it was

i started facing reality
no longer threatened by
the blind spots and weaknesses that remained

life was for learning and i was in school
eventually i figured out the value
of changing some of my behaviors
and attitudes and
in spite of myself
i grew up

the reward

i realized
i had not been abandoned
and i never walked alone
no matter what the circumstances were
that brought me into this world
and no matter what my life experiences had been
i had an active part
in the unfolding of humanity and the earth
for better or worse

it was up to me
to decide what kind of a world i lived in
and what kind of a world i left behind

i was freed
from the grief i struggled with all of my life
because i finally understood
that all of life was precious
even mine

i stopped waiting for love and approval
and decided to live without pretense
and it was then
that my liberation was complete

i wasn't responsible for changing
anyone or anything
except me
i found that struggling to reach an understanding
with those who were determined
to fortify their own delusions
at my expense
cost too much
life was a miracle
and i did not intend on wasting one minute of it
so i didn't

i stopped trying to determine who the gardener was
and instead

the reward

simply
delighted in being a flower
planted for a while
in this amazing garden

and i realized
that a life well shared
was its own reward

down the road

26. years later

my children are grown now
our relationships continue to be
loving respectful gracious and honest
we know life is precious and we keep having
way too much fun
living it

i still enjoy
expressing on paper and canvas
the guts of
all of it
and quietly share life with my
bodacious family
a few dear friends
and my service dog coco

i have learned how to keep a safe distance
from the distractions that clever charmers
and directors of chaos
tend to bring into our lives

and i appreciate living in peace

i finally got the courage
to go back to college
to finish what i started back in 1972
and in 2005
on the dean's list
i graduated from columbia college in chicago

these days coco and i travel
outside these walls
and we help people in need

i did not know how far
down the road
i was going to go

years later

but i learned
that the journey was never about
getting there
it was about how we lived
along the way

i am not as reclusive as i once was
i remain
here and now
gratefully connected

my questions have been answered
yours are your own
the only words of wisdom i have left are these
live honorably
give love freely
think for yourself
never let other people define who you are
and enjoy the trip
it's all yours

ziji*

*ziji is tibetan for windhorse and it means:
to ride the energy of our existence,
powered by our basic goodness;
i read this in the book,
"shambhala - the sacred path of the warrior"
it was written by chogyam trungpa

Made in the USA
Lexington, KY
11 May 2014